Unprecedented
Press

The Best Kids Explore Ontario © 2025 by Joshua Best

All rights reserved. No part of this publication may be reproduced, distributed, or transmitted in any form or by any means, including photocopying, recording, or other electronic or mechanical methods, without the prior written permission of the publisher or author, except in the case of brief quotations embodied in critical reviews and certain other noncommercial uses permitted by copyright law. For permission requests, email the publisher or author at addresses below:

Contact the publisher:
Unprecedented Press LLC - 229 W Main Ave, Zeeland, MI 49464
www.unprecedentedpress.com | info@unprecedentedpress.com
instagram: unprecedentedpress

ISBN: 979-8-9867126-3-5

Ingram Printing & Distribution, 2025

First Edition

— the — BEST KIDS — explore —

FEATURING: maps, reviews, travel tips, and true tales of family adventures

ONTARIO

An illustrated, story-driven travel guide for kids

CONTENTS

MEET THE KIDS 4
LODGING & TRANSPORT 6
STORIES:

WHAT COMES AROUND 8
in Niagara Falls, ON

PUMPKINS & PEANUTS 18
in Vaughan, ON

UP, UP & AWAY 24
in Toronto, ON

LET YOUR HAIR DOWN 32
in Ottawa, ON

LITTLE DETAILS 38
BEST BITES 39
BEST BETS 40
BUMPS IN THE ROAD 42

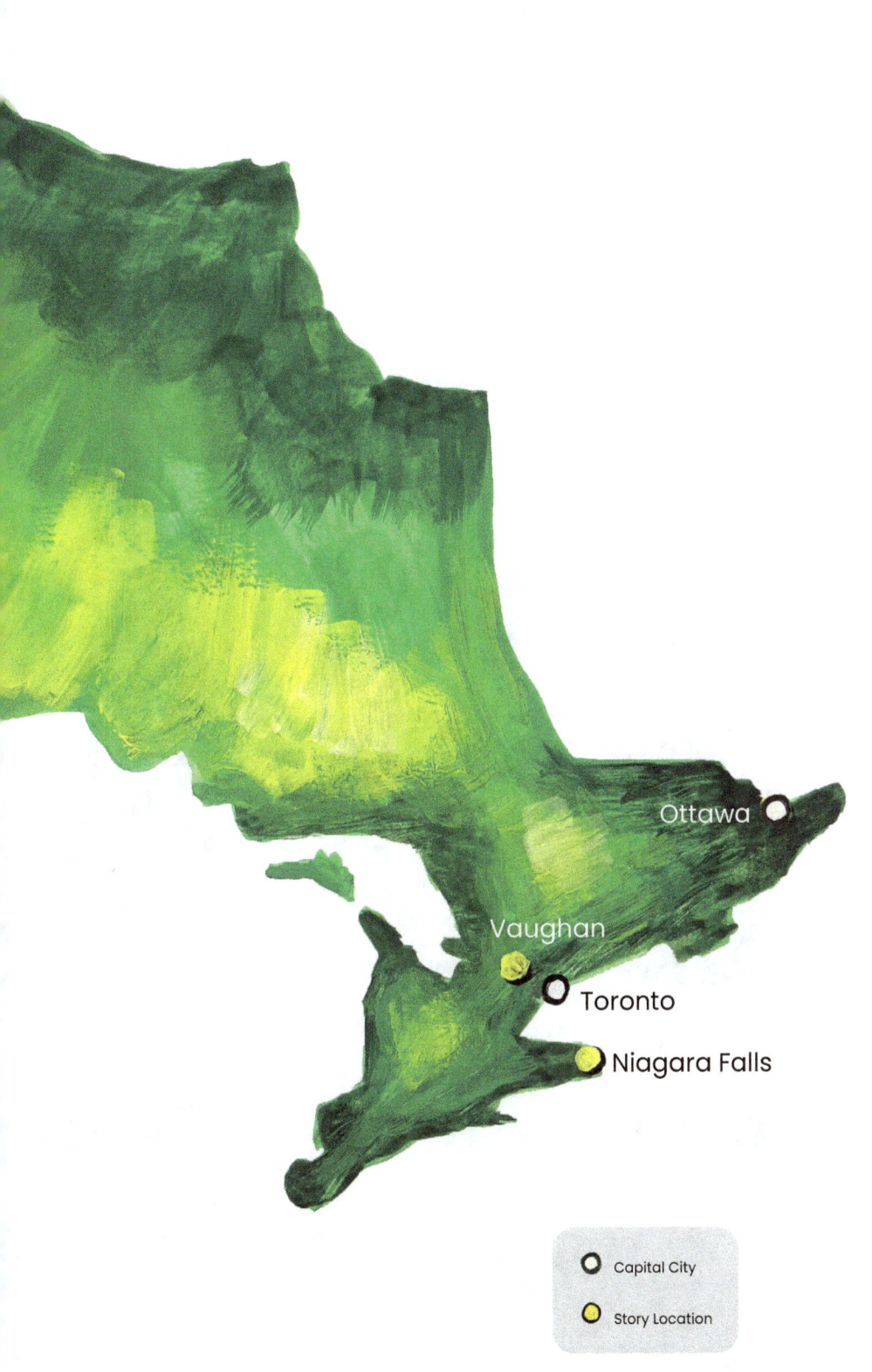

MEET THE KIDS

Exploring is the best. Exploring lets you discover the cool things around you – things you didn't know were there before. That's what makes it so much fun! It's exciting to find out what's around the corner, across the border and beyond the horizon.

The Best kids are explorers. They love finding new places to play and discovering new ways to have fun. The oldest is Frederick – he has orange hair. The middle child is Edith – she has brown hair. The youngest is Hugo – he has yellow hair. The Best kids are half American and half Canadian. They live in Michigan.

In this book, the kids travel to the Canadian province of Ontario. At the time of their expedition, Frederick was nine years old, Edith was seven years old, and Hugo was four years old. This trip occurred between the months of May and June.

LODGING & TRANSPORT

The Best family traveled to Ontario by car – by way of their grey Chevy Traverse to be exact. With snacks packed, movies downloaded to watch and rest stops planned, they traveled east across Michigan. They reached the border in Port Huron and crossed into Canada on the Bluewater Bridge. Their journey picked up in Sarnia, Ontario, and they continued southeast past the city of London and onto their first destination – Niagara Falls.

FAIRFIELD INN & SUITES

For lodging, the kids stayed at the Fairfield Inn & Suites in downtown Niagara Falls. Later, they reached the Residence Inn in Vaughan, which was their homebase for visiting Canada's Wonderland and downtown Toronto.

In Ottawa, they stayed at The Groenewegs' house. The Groenewegs are good friends of the Best kids' parents, and they have three kids of their own: Lily, Malachi and Vinny. This was the best lodging of all because it came with good friends, tons of toys, and lots of laughs.

WHAT COMES AROUND

On a pleasant spring day, it was Papa's birthday. This year was a milestone, so the Best kids' extended family were coming together to celebrate. But it wasn't just going to be a party – it was a surprise party. And it wasn't just going to be at home – everyone was meeting up in Niagara Falls.

Like with every road trip, the Best kids packed their bags, and hit the road nice and early. They drove east across the state of Michigan and across the Bluewater Bridge into Ontario. After showing their passports, they were granted entry by the border patrol officers. Everything was going smoothly!

Minutes later, their dad called out, "Something's dinging!"

It was the dashboard alerting him that one of their tires was losing air pressure. All of the Bests looked at each other with worried expressions on their faces. What does that mean? What was going to happen?

"Let's pull over near the mall up ahead and figure out what we should do." said their mom.

So, their dad got off the highway and turned into a nearby strip mall with a sprinkling of big box stores. There, they got out to check the tire, and yes they had in fact, run over a nail. Immediately, the family discussed finding a mechanic shop to fix the tire and continue on their journey, but before they had a chance to look on their phones, Frederick pointed out the window, exclaiming, "Isn't that a tire shop?!"

He was pointing at Canadian Tire, a well known hardware chain in Canada which also sells home goods and auto parts. Apparently, they got a flat tire at the best possible spot, so they pulled up to the store.

With a fresh patch, and some

snacks from inside, the Best kids were back on the road. They were so excited to see their cousins and their grandparents!

As they approached the city of Niagara Falls, they passed through numerous small towns where the speed limit dropped momentarily. In one of those small towns, their dad didn't see the sign, and drove through the village too quickly. The error would have gone unnoticed if it weren't for the police officer, waiting in his patrol car on the outskirts of town. The sound of a siren made everyone nervous, but their mom told them not to worry. The policeman issued their dad a speeding ticket and asked him to be safer next time.

Now with two driving incidents in the rearview mirror,

the Best family was tired of driving. Finally, they arrived in Niagara Falls!

Quickly, the kids hauled their luggage into the elevator at Fairfield Inn and suites. On the third floor, they met their cousins Lucy and Anna, their Uncle Luke, and their Aunt Sarah who were staying there too. Everyone scrambled or to unpack their bags because Nana and Papa would arrive any minute, and Papa didn't know the kids were coming. In fact, he was told he was having a meeting with some colleagues.

With a text alert from Nana, they waited in their rooms while Nana and Papa settled into theirs. Quietly, both families crept across the hall, opened the door to their grandparents' hotel room, and yelled, "Surprise!"

Papa was so happy to see them and celebrate together! After reuniting, they went to check out the falls!

Together, the family walked from their hotel room and along the Niagara River Parkway, a scenic walk up to the waterfalls. On the way up, they stopped for a photo in front of the beautiful, booming water and the orange, setting sun.

At the top of the lookout, there were ponchos offered to visitors because of how much mist came off the falls. The Best kids didn't mind getting a little wet, so they skipped the ponchos. It was amazing to watch the powerful river drop off the side of a cliff with such force! It was thunderous and mesmerizing.

Once they had sufficiently explored the falls and the gift shop, the Best kids and their extended family wandered back down the pathway towards Clifton Hill.

What they didn't realize was that the wind had changed directions, and was now blowing an enormous cloud of mist right onto them! This is what the ponchos were for! This wasn't a few drops; their backs were getting drenched as they ran away in the opposite direction, laughing their heads off!

Clifton Hill is the *Las Vegas-style* strip of Niagara Falls. Everywhere you look, there are flashing lights, carnival, games, and tasty treats. The Best kids settled for a single slice in a triangular box from Pizza Pizza for dinner, and made their way over to the Niagara Sky Wheel.

Standing at over seventeen stories tall, this massive ferris wheel can be quite intimidating. As they got closer and waited in line, the kids started to have second thoughts.

"Are you sure it's safe?" asked Edith.

"How long do we have to stay in there?" asked Hugo.

Once they got to the front of the line and stepped

inside of the pod, they discovered it was heated, played soothing music, had lighting control, and it could seat up to nine people! Unfortunately, all of these bells and whistles didn't make it any less scary.

As the ride began, and the wheel started turning, their pod began to rock back-and-forth, which freaked them out! It took them higher and higher, and eventually they could see the falls. But this time, it was dark and they falls were lit up with colorful lights. Amazing!

After going around three or four times, and wondering if they would ever set their feet on the ground ever again, the ride finally stopped. It was nerve-racking, but it was fun!

The kids gathered their thoughts and talked about the ride over a strawberry funnel cake, which their dad bought nearby.

Niagara Falls had a few surprises, but no matter what happened, they knew as long as they had each other, they would always land on their feet.

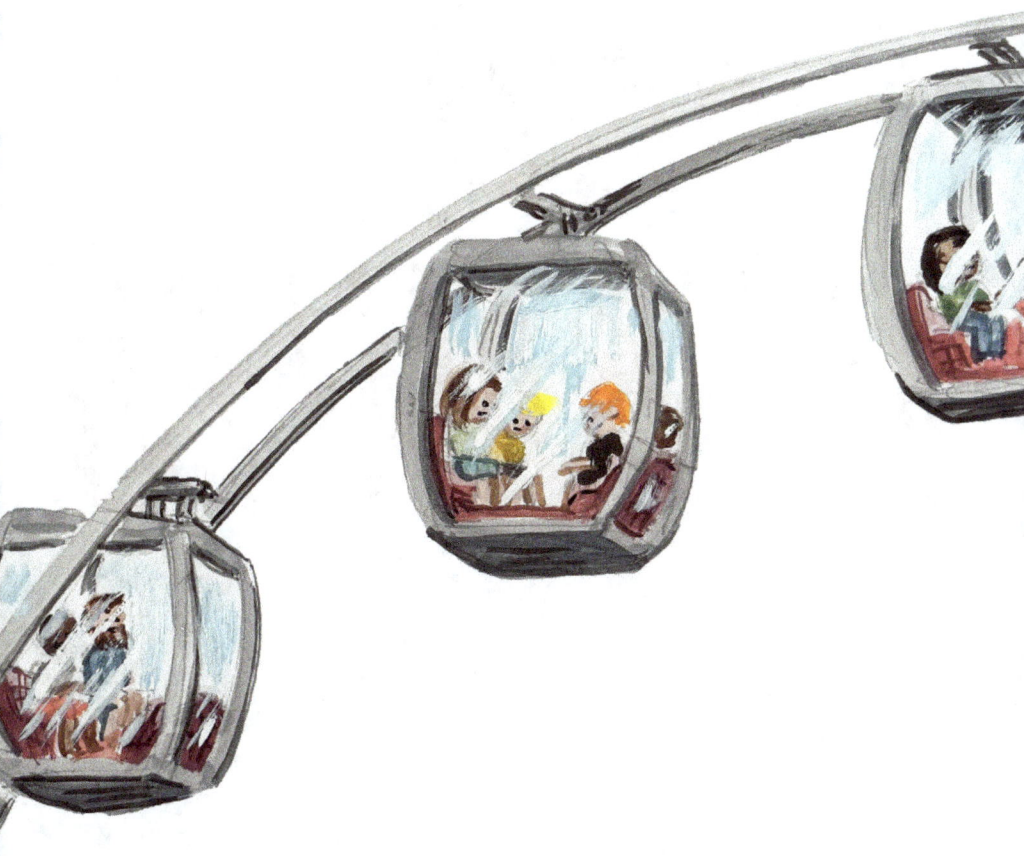

PUMPKINS AND PEANUTS

Sitting in front of a pile of trash, the Best family was coming to terms with the post-Covid, free hotel breakfast. It wasn't as good as it once was, but they didn't care because their hotel was minutes away from Canada's Wonderland – Ontario's preeminent theme park.

They quickly gathered their things, jumped in the car, and were getting excited as they approached the gates – except for the Best kids' mom. She had been here as a teenager and threw up on a ride! She was still willing to come, but she didn't want to go on any rides.

Once inside the park, they noticed the classic roller coaster Dragon's Fyre had a short line. They split up so the big kids could ride it. Frederick and Edith were so

worried about going upside down for the first time that they didn't consider the epic hill at the beginning of the ride. They loved it, and walked off the coaster with wide eyes and hair blown.

Frederick, Edith and dad quickly met back up with Hugo and mom in the Peanuts themed area for kids. Hugo had ridden one small ride, but was gearing up for the big one in this area called Boo Blasters.

"Do you guys want to go on this ghost ride?" Hugo asked the other two.

They agreed enthusiastically and ran to line up. Inside, they were carted through a dark haunted house, and shot creepy characters with green laser guns. Hugo loved it!

The kids continued exploring the park. They flew on Snoopy's airplanes, cruised

in Woodstock's boat, and had their picture taken with Peppermint Patty.

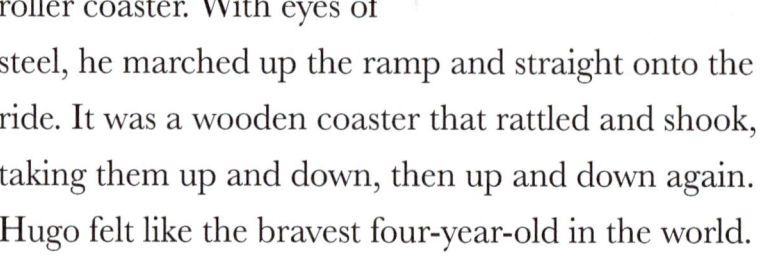

While their mom picked up lunch at a nearby diner, the rest of them stood at the entrance of the Ghoster Coaster – another spooky ride, and Hugo's first roller coaster. With eyes of steel, he marched up the ramp and straight onto the ride. It was a wooden coaster that rattled and shook, taking them up and down, then up and down again. Hugo felt like the bravest four-year-old in the world.

In the afternoon, Frederick looked at his mom and asked, "Are you really not going to ride *any* rides? Not even one?"

His mom was quiet for a moment. They could see her trying to overcome her distaste for rides.

"Okay! I'll try one." she conceded.

The kids cheered and looked around for a low intensity ride their mom could handle. Beside the bumper cars, they spotted Linus's Pumpkin Patch, a bright orange ride that lifted you up slowly into the air. Perfect for mom!

As the ride began, the kids' dad stayed below and took pictures. As they floated through the air in the orange pumpkins, the kids realized that even grown-ups find it hard to be brave sometimes. They were so proud of their mom!

UP, UP, UP AND AWAY

On the outskirts of the city, the Best kids walked across the street to the subway station. It was not only their first time riding the TTC (Toronto Transit Comission), it was their first time on a subway train!

They bought a Family Day Pass at the kiosk in the station, and entered through the turnstile. Taking the escalator deep underground was thrilling and eerie at the same time. After waiting for only a couple of minutes, they heard a rumbling sound, and they saw a light shining in the distance. It grew larger and larger until a train burst through the dark tunnel, and came to a screeching halt right in front of them. The doors opened wide, and after other people stepped out, they ran in and grabbed the railings. When the door closed, the subway car jolted forward making Frederick, Edith and Hugo lose their balance.

As the Best family wrote the subway train, the kids learned how to accommodate the backward and

25

forward motions, as well as the sharp turns. By the end of the journey, they were riding the train like surfers on a big wave.

They got off at Union Station, Toronto's central hub. From there, they walked through a skywalk to reach the CN Tower. The Canadian National Tower is one of the largest freestanding structures in the world, and held the record for the tallest at one point. It is the most iconic part of Toronto's skyline and one of the main attractions in the city.

After passing through security, they reached the elevator which skyrocketed them upwards 114 storeys up into

the air. The elevator had windows for them to see how high they were going, which was captivating, but also terrifying! Finally, they reached the main deck. Their first instinct was to find the windows and look out, but as they walked over, they also found windows on the floor!

It's not common to walk on glass, so this was pretty scary! But the kids took turns daring each other and posing for photos on the glass floor.

The CN Tower was a marvel! And the view was unrivaled. There's nothing in the city of Toronto you couldn't see from the lookout. Later, the kids went up to the highest observation deck (another 33 storeys up)

called the Sky Pod, where they could actually feel the tower moving slightly with the motion of the wind.

The next activity in Toronto was meeting up with Uncle Jamo and Uncle Tobiasz who live in the city. They invited them to eat lunch at a Thai restaurant called Salad King. It was well known in the city, had delicious food, and fantastic decor! Frederick came back to the table from the restaurant bathroom and said, "You have to check out the stairwell!"

Before they left the restaurant, they each went down to the bathroom to see an intricate mirror installation, where murals were reflected in amazing ways!

The next stop for the Best kids was Chinatown, but instead of walking there, they waited on the street corner for a streetcar, which is like a bus, but it runs on a track in the road, and it's powered by an electrical connection high above.

"Ding, ding, ding!"

The street car pulled up in front of them, and after scanning their day passes, the kids boarded.

They rode for nine blocks, and the kids' dad said,

"Edith, do you want to pull the cord?"

Once he explained that pulling a small, yellow cord on the wall of a streetcar alerts the driver to let you off, she agreed with excitement. "Yes, please!"

She pulled the cord, and the kids were instantly transported to a place that looked like a different country! The kids loved exploring Chinatown: the shops, the smell of unkown foods, and the unique, affordable trinkets from street vendors.

With Thai food in their bellies, and Chinese culture all around, their uncle suggested, one more cultural experience – bubble tea (or boba tea as some people call it). So, on the way to Uncle Jamo and Uncle Tobiasz's apartment, they stopped at a Taiwanese bubble tea stand and ordered their favorite flavors.

Frederick got passionfruit tea with mandarin bobas,

Edith got lemon tea with brown sugar bobas, and Hugo doubled down on strawberry tea with strawberry bobas.

As they sat on the balcony of their uncles' apartment indulging in this Taiwanese treat, they reflected on their shifting points of view. They noted how riding an underground train and ascending a soaring tower helped them see the world from a new perspective.

LET YOUR HAIR DOWN

The Best kids arrived in Ottawa, Ontario at the end of their trip. It was their last destination, and they had been away for some time. Not only were they missing home, but they were also starting to look a bit shaggy!

The plan was to stay with some friends of their parents called the Groenewegs. Thankfully, they had kids of similar ages: Lily, Malachi and Vinny.

When they first arrived, they had a great dinner together and played in their backyard where they had bikes, trikes, and lightsabers! Meanwhile, the two

dads talked about the journey up to this point, and how much Hugo needed a haircut. Just minutes later they brought the hair clippers outside.

In the midst of a backyard lightsaber battle, Hugo got a five minute haircut.

With a new morning came a new plan. Ottawa is the capital city of Canada, so they went downtown to explore the sights. The first stop was the Peace Tower on Parliament Hill, the centerpiece of Canada's federal government campus. In front of the tower was the Centennial Flame, a fire that hasn't gone out since Canada turned 100 years old in 1967. Both were majestic to look at, but there was a fair amount of walking to reach it, so Edith was geting *hangry*.

From there, the kids and their newfound friends walked down the street a little further to the Château Laurier,

a hotel that looks like a castle. Mrs. Groeneweg, who is originally from England noted that Queen Elizabeth stayed at the Château Laurier when she visited Ottawa. They considered sitting down for a fancy English tea party, but on this day they opted for a more informal choice – BeaverTails.

The two families continued their walk toward Byward Market, a popular destination for shoppers and foodies visiting Ottawa. They had their eyes, hearts and stomachs set on stopping at the famous Canadian snack spot called BeaverTails.

They pulled up with their strollers, gazed upon the

elaborate menu featuring a wide array of sugary delights on fried dough. After some debate, they landed on a cookies n' cream BeaverTail, and a chocolate with peanut butter BeaverTail topped off with Reese's Pieces.

The two families found a place to sit and share the chocolatey, peanut-buttery deliciousness. With more of it on their faces than in their bellies, the kids ran across the plaza to play and climb on six gigantic letters, spelling out the word, "OTTAWA". Although the Best kids were born in the United States, they're also Canadian, and the joy they found in Ottawa with the Groeneweg family made them feel right at home.

LITTLE DETAILS

SUNGLASSES AT KENSINGTON MARKET

The kids loved shopping for tchotchkes in Chinatown and at Kensington Market. One sidewalk sale had thousands of eccentric pairs of sunglasses, which were fun to try on!

OCAD WINDOWS

In between destinations, the Best kids walked to their dads old campus at the Ontario College of Art and Design. It was a building built on stilts above another building! The stilts looked like giant colored pencils, and the kids we able to sit inside of the deep neon-colored windows on the top floor.

STUNT COASTER

When the kids' mom took the younger two to see a friend, Frederick and his dad got to ride the Stunt Coaster at Canada's Wonderland. Based on the movie *The Italian Job*, it was very fast – a real highlight!

BEST BITES

SALAD KING

In downtown Toronto, Uncle Jamo and Uncle Tobiasz took the Best family to a Thai food restuarant near their dad's college. The name made it sound like their speciality was salad, but it wasn't – just spicy, delicious Thai food. A great experience!

BEAVER TAILS

No tourist's trip to Canada is complete without a visit to BeaverTails. If you like Elephant Ears, try this sweet destination!

PIZZA PIZZA

Ubiquitous but not gourmet by any means, Pizza Pizza is a great quick stop for a large, single slice. The kids loved the triangular orange box it was served in.

BEST BETS

NIAGARA FALLS
NIAGARA FALLS, ON

The walk to the Horseshoe Falls was inspiring and the great mist that overtook the kids on the walk back was unexpected.

CANADA'S WONDERLAND
VAUGHAN, ON

This is a great theme park. Busy, yes. But filled with great rides and also well-maintained.

BYWARD MARKET
OTTAWA, ON

A happening place downtown with great restaurants, and good photo opportunities.

CN TOWER
TORONTO, ON

An epic elevator ride rockets you 147 storeys into the air, and the view from the top is unbelievable.

CHINATOWN & KENSINGTON MARKET
TORONTO, ON

This downtown retail area was super authentic and offered unique buys.

BUMPS IN THE ROAD

TTC DETOUR

At one point, while riding the subway, the kids discovered they would have to switch over to a bus for a segment of the ride. They were doing maintenance work on the tracks for a segment of their route. It made for an extra long ride, and a an extra big headache.

SPEEDING TICKET & FLAT TIRE

The Best kids' dad was super embarassed about being pulled over for speeding – not his finest moment. At least the officer was kind about it! And thankfully their vehicle alerted them to the flat tire with enough time for them to fix it at Canadian Tire.

HEIGHT RESTRICTIONS

One challenging detail at Canada's Wonderland were the kids' varying heights. Like most theme parks, ride access is determined by how tall you are. With five years between Frederick and Hugo, they had a height differential of nearly twelve inches, so the Best family often needed to split into groups to go on the rides.

ABOUT THE AUTHOR

The adventures of the Best kids found on these pages were chronicled by none other than their own father. Joshua Best is a writer, and illustrator by night. By day, he is a creative director at a marketing agency. Of all these roles, there is none better than being a dad to Frederick, Edith and Hugo.

FOLLOW ALONG

Why wait until the next book is released when you can find out now where the kids are headed? Follow the kids on Instagram to watch illustration in progress and to see real photos of current trips! Also, check out the website for ways to get in touch, or listen to our podcast on Spotify, Google or Apple Podcasts.

 @thebestkids_explore

 @thebestkids_explore

 thebestkidsexplore.com

 The Best Kids Explore

www.ingramcontent.com/pod-product-compliance
Lightning Source LLC
Chambersburg PA
CBHW050521100526
44581CB00002B/63

Life Is Just a Dream
A Book of Poetry

As Told By Lucky Goldie

Poetic Production NYC
Brooklyn, New York

Copyright © 2025 by Decorey Linton

Writing as Lucky Goldie

All rights reserved. No part of this publication may be reproduced, distributed, or transmitted in any form or by any means, including photocopying, recording, or other electronic or mechanical methods, without the prior written permission of the publisher, except in the case of brief quotations embodied in critical reviews and certain other noncommercial uses permitted by copyright law.

Published by Poetic Production NYC

Brooklyn, New York

www.PoeticProductionNYC.com

ISBN: 979-8-9990401-5-2

Library of Congress Control Number: Pending Assignment

This is a work of poetry. Any resemblance to actual persons, living or dead, or actual events is purely coincidental or used in artistic expression.

For permissions or inquiries, please contact:

DLamont100@yahoo.com

First Edition

Registered with the United States Copyright Office

Registration Number: TXu 2-479-782

Effective Date: February 28, 2025

Table of Contents

Dedication	PG 3
Introduction	PG 4
Section 1: Eternal Youth & Innocence	PG 7-11
Section 2: Rhythms of Hip Hop and Justice	PG 12-16
Section 3: The Tales Of... (Chronologically Arranged)	PG 17-26
Section 4: Strength and Resilience	PG 27-31
Section 5: Love, Honor, and Loyalty	PG 32-35
Section 6: Life's Cycles and Seasons	PG 36-39
Section 7: Reflection on Wealth and Purpose	PG 40-45
Section 8: Faith, Legacy, and Guidance	PG 46-50
Acknowledgemnts	PG 51
About the Author	PG 52

Dedication:

To my dear beloved brother, Sheron Michael "Moe" Linton (December 16, 1986 - June 9, 2013), A remarkable warrior, a timeless legend, your memory is etched in poetic infinity. You walked this earth with grace and strength, leaving behind a legacy that transcends time. Your spirit is the heartbeat of this book, the light that guides every word. You taught me resilience, love, and the power of dreams. Though you've gone on, your presence remains, whispering through the lines, blessing every page. This is for you, Moe, my brother, my muse, my eternal inspiration. Bless up, brother. Forever in my heart.

Introduction:

Life is Just a Dream invites you into a world where words reflect life's journey—the highs, the lows, the struggles, and the victories. This collection is more than poetry; it's a testament to resilience, a celebration of love, and a call to honor the strength within each of us. Each poem is rooted in experiences both personal and universal, speaking to the beauty of growth, the courage to rise, and the wisdom gained along the way.

The poems in these pages cover a range of themes: from the rhythms of hip hop that pulse through our lives, to stories of loss and remembrance, to the tales of ordinary moments that shape extraordinary lives. With each line, I hope to remind you that we are all navigating dreams, striving to hold onto the essence of who we are in a world that often feels like a mix of wonder and mystery.

As you read, my wish is that these words resonate with your own journey. May they bring you solace, spark memories, or inspire you to keep dreaming, no matter the challenges. Life, after all, is just a dream—fragile, fleeting, yet full of meaning.

Bless up,
Lucky Goldie

Poetry Content:

Section 1: Eternal Youth & Innocence
Life is just a Dream
Twin Forces of Life
Bound by Love, Called by Destiny
The Price of Gold

Section 2: Rhythms of Justice and Hip Hop
I Do It for Hip Hop
A Tale from Sedgwick to Wu
Poetic Justice in Motion
Brooklyn's Finest

Section 3: The Tales of Life
The Tale of Eternal Youth
The Tale of the Young Lover
The Tale of a Brave Soul
The Tale of Fatherhood
The Tale of Seasons
Epiphany Ignited
The Golden Soldier
Winds of the Water Bearer
The Dance of Yin and Yang

Section 4: Resilience and Strength
Courage in Motion
Stand Tall, Keep Going
Breaking the Chains
Seasons of Gold

Poetry Content:

Section 5: Love, Honor, and Connection
Love Unconditionally
Lukewarm Balance
The Power of Patience

Section 6: Life's Cycles and Humanity
Dear Summer, Dear Winter
The Dance of Change
From Struggle to Trust

Section 7 : Reflections on Wealth and Purpose
Beyond the Money Game
Dreams of Decadence
The Bigger Picture
In the Quiet of Greatness
Riches in Spirit

Section 8: Faith and Legacy
The Vision Alive
Written in the Stars
Seeking Eternal Truth
The Truth of Love

Section 1: Eternal Youth Innocence

Reflection

Exploring the magic of innocence, resilience, and the lasting spirit of youth.

"Life Is Just a Dream"
Peace, Love, and Blessings My Beloved Family and Friends

Life is but a canvas painted with time,
a fleeting masterpiece, both surreal and sublime.
From the laughter of youth to the echoes of years,
it cradles our joy, it embraces our fears.
Eternal youth—no, it never departs,
it lives in our soul, it beats in our hearts.

Do you remember your childhood flame?
A favorite toy, a beloved game?
The songs that played as the days rolled by,
or the first time a movie made you cry?
These memories linger, they shimmer and gleam,
reminding us softly: life is just a dream.

From boys to men, from girls to queens,
we chase the horizon, we craft new scenes.
Yet beneath the layers, that spark remains,
a child's wonder, untouched by life's chains.
It hides, it waits, beneath life's stream,
to remind us again—life is just a dream.

And then, the miracle: we create anew,
a child born, a piece of you.
In their eyes, you see the spark ignite,
a reflection of you, a beacon of light.
Time folds in on itself, a perfect scheme,
proving once more—life is just a dream.

The risks, the rewards, the wonder, the pain,
the balance of sunshine and the cleansing rain.
The yin, the yang, the push, the pull,
the mysteries vast, the universe full.
From the bird's-eye view, it all aligns,
a cosmic dance through space and time.

This fleeting life, it's a gift, you see,
a blend of wonder and mystery.
So hold on tight to the spark you glean,
and never forget—life is just a dream.

Is this poetry in motion, or poetic justice?
I ask because the dream feels so real,
and yet, it's the awe and wonder we steal—
proof that even in the fleeting, there's eternal truth,
a cycle of innocence, a cycle of youth.

Yours Truly,
The Dreamcatcher of Words,
Lucky Goldie

Peace, love, and blessings, my beloved family and friends,

Two forces rise within us all, unseen yet strong,
Estrogen and testosterone—each a powerful song.
Estrogen, the essence of grace, soft yet fierce,
It nurtures, it creates, holds life so dear.
It flows like water, gentle but deep,
Building mountains where the heart dares to leap.
The power to bear, to heal, to renew,
A strength unmatched, but quiet and true.

Testosterone, the fire, bold and brave,
A force that drives, that conquers the wave.
It builds and protects, fights for the cause,
With unshaken will, never seeking applause.
Muscle and might, the essence of drive,
Fueling ambition, keeping the spirit alive.
It roars like thunder, impossible to ignore,
Breaking boundaries, always asking for more.

But what if we see beyond the surface, past the veil,
That both these powers together never fail?
One molds the earth, the other sparks the flame,
Both in harmony, never quite the same.
The void within, the space we all feel,
Can cloud the truth, can make us forget what's real.
For estrogen whispers, and testosterone shouts,
But together they conquer all our doubts.

Awe-inspiring forces, the balance of life,
Each with its role, each causing strife—
Yet, it's in their union we find our truth,
The essence of creation, eternal youth.
Both powers hold the world in their hands,
Guiding us through time, shaping the lands.
To see this bigger picture, to feel it all,
Is to embrace the rise, before we fall.

The moral, my beloved, is this:
We are all filled with power, with grace, and with fire,
And only together can we rise higher.
Estrogen and testosterone, the twin forces of might,
In awe we stand, blessed by their light.

Is this poetry in motion, or is it poetic justice?
Yours truly,
Lucky Goldie.

Peace, love, and blessings, my beloved family and friends,

Let me speak to the real, unlike any other. From young boys to men, life threw us in deep, With dreams still bound, but the stakes run steep.

I've watched you grow, your cadence a fire, Spitting words that lift, a lyrical sire. A prolific force, yet your light's held back, Bound to Momma's fears, caught up in her lack.

See, life's been cruel, we both know it well, Our father vanished, Moe's story fell. Through silence and scars, we've shouldered the weight, Yet somehow, you're trapped by a bond you can't break.

All that talent, raw, untouched, unshown, But you're grown now, bro, it's time to own. I moved mountains for you, put you on that stage, Yet last-minute fears left plans disengaged.

I get it, I do—your spirit feels torn, Between the comfort you know, and the crown you were born. Momma raised us strong but clutches you tight, Holding you close, yet dimming your light.

This ain't a curse, little brother, it's a call, Rise above the weight, stand proud, stand tall. Because the world needs to hear what you got to say, Don't let your gift be the one that got away.

It's not too late to claim what's yours, Step out of the shadows, through opened doors. Look around, the family's fractured and weak, But you're stronger than silence, stand firm, don't speak.

For in you lies a legacy bold, unbent, Unseen, unbroken, a talent heaven-sent. A momma's boy maybe, but man, don't stall, Pick up your crown, don't let it fall.

Is this poetry in motion, or is it poetic justice?

Yours truly,
Lucky Goldie

Peace, love, and blessings, my beloved family and friends,

This here tale unfolds with gold glimmers, but no end, A world of money, power, respect on high, Yet its price, hidden deep, few can deny.

See, money whispers promises bold and bright, Luring men and women into the night, It's tantalizing, hypnotic, a siren's call, But many have stumbled, heedless of the fall.

Power's a rush, a taste so sweet, Yet it demands a loyalty you can't unseat, And in the mirror, reflections fade, For in this lust, innocence is betrayed.

Respect comes with chains; it's no gift, it's a loan, One false move, and it's gone—you're alone, And sex, a spell cast in heat and fire, Yet too often it burns, unquenchable desire.

And what of the drugs that numb the soul? A temporary high, a mirage of control, They promise escape but leave you bound, In this gilded trap, where dreams are drowned.

Each chase, each grasp, for what seems like bliss, Leaves behind scars, a toxic abyss. My beloved, heed this humble request: The treasures that tempt us may fail the test.

The moral's simple, family and friends, Know your worth, for gold fades in the end.

Is this poetry in motion, or is it poetic justice?

Yours truly,
Lucky Goldie

Section 2: Rhythms of Hip Hop and Justice

Reflection

A tribute to the power of hip hop where rhythm meets justice, eching through time.

Peace, love, and blessings, my beloved family and friends,

From the heart of hip hop to the soul of rhyme,
"I Do It For Hip Hop" echoes back through time.
Ludacris, Jay, and Nas—kings of the craft,
Each bar they spit, every lyric they draft,
Is poetry in motion, from the booth to the beat,
A melody alive, a rhythm complete.
They move mountains with verbs and nouns,
Raise up our spirits, tear down our bounds.
Every verse written, every word is a sign,
That hip hop and poetry are deeply aligned.

And then there's Poetic Justice, raw and true,
Pac and Janet painted emotions in hues,
Captured love and pain in every glance,
Through struggles and journeys, given the chance
To speak of worlds that most can't see,
Of love's sweet ache and fierce destiny.
Every scene crafted, every line so pure,
This was more than a film; it was love's cure.
In moments of tension, in words unspoken,
Justice found its way through hearts unbroken.

This is why I say it, why I end my rhyme—
"Is this poetry in motion?" moving through time.
Or "Is this poetic justice?" a truth, a release,
A way to find beauty, a way to find peace.
For the essence of poetry, be it rap or verse,
Is to speak to the soul, to heal or to curse.
Like hip hop's heartbeat or love's gentle grace,
These words are a mirror, a time, and a place.

So when I say it, I'm asking you all,
Do these words lift you up, or answer the call?
Is it rhythm that drives, or justice that reigns,
Or maybe both, like love and its pains?
Because poetry is motion—a force to ignite,
And justice? It's truth, it's vision, it's light.

The moral is simple, my family and friends:
We find ourselves through the verses we pen.
Is this poetry in motion, or is it poetic justice?

Yours truly,
Lucky Goldie.

Peace, love, and blessings, my beloved family and friends,

From Sedgwick Ave, where it all began,
To Bucktown, where kings took a stand,
County of Kings made a fair exchange,
With the County of Queens, hip hop's range.

Past the 59 bridge to Money Makin' Manhattan,
Now we walkin' dogs on Wu Island, what's happenin'?
Hip hop's DNA embedded deep in the earth,
Setting trends for ages, defining our worth.

When hip hop sneezes, the whole world catches the cold,
Live from your living room radio, stories unfold.
Headphones booming, from your favorite ride,
Still rockin' "No I can't live without my radio" pride.

We came from Mama Africa, shackled, breaker of chains,
Saw greatness that awaited, patient, bold gains.
Conquered slavery, foresaw our story's unfold,
Naturally pushed to conquer, our greatness gold.

Now the world leans on the black brain, no doubt,
Godspeed at its finest, our spirit's devout.
We shall overcome, and overcame we did,
Bless up to the stars and back, we outlived.

Hip hop's power, live and direct,
From your speakers to the streets, feel the effect.
The moral's simple, family and friends,
We've conquered all, the story transcends.

Is this poetry in motion, or is it poetic justice?
Bless up my beloved, let's keep this energy illustrious.

Yours truly,
Lucky Goldie.

Peace, love, and blessings, my beloved family and friends,

We came from the bottom, razor sharp, cuttin' through strife
Lloyd and Meth said it best—"101 razors" is the life.
We had nothing but hunger, the grind in our veins,
Turning water to wine, pushin' through the pain.
Ish to sugar, from the dirt we rise,
Ashy to classy, now the whole world's surprised.

No silver spoons, just knives in our hands,
We carved out a future, made our own plans.
America wasn't built for kids like us,
But we flipped the script, turned struggle to trust.
Every scar on my skin, every tear in my soul,
Only sharpened the blade, made me more in control.

See, we never had much, but we had heart,
From the concrete jungle, we played our part.
The block was cold, the nights even colder,
But now we sit back, heads high on our shoulders.
We embraced the struggle, never let it defeat,
Now it's champagne toasts every time we eat.

From the cracks of the street to the shine of success,
We learned how to move, we learned how to finesse.
We made it, family, we broke through the chains,
Turned pain into power, our hustle remains.

The moral here, beloved, is clear and just,
In this life, you must push, you must trust.
From the grind to the shine, it's all part of the plan,
We made it in America—take a bow, fam.

Is this poetry in motion, or is it poetic justice?

Yours truly,
Lucky Goldie.

Peace, love, and blessings, my beloved family and friends,

In a world so twisted, we rise from the dirt,
Kings once crowned, now questioning their worth.
Jay said it best, "The same sword they knight you with,
They'll good night you with"—that's how the world shifts.
We stand tall, wearing crowns made of thorns,
But behind the gold and glory, we're often torn.

They cheer when you rise, but plot when you fall,
It's madness out here—who's real after all?
The same hands that clap for you will tighten the noose,
Jealousy, envy, in silence let loose.
But we move like shadows, swift and precise,
Navigating the madness, paying the price.

The sword they gave me, I sharpened with pain,
Turned every loss into wisdom gained.
But even kings feel the weight of the crown,
Some days we fly, some days we drown.
Fortune may forsake us, the gold may fade,
But through the chaos, we've made the grade.

And so, we push forward with iron in our veins,
Forged through the struggle, we break the chains.
No longer bound by the world's deceit,
We walk light, my family, we'll never retreat.

The moral here, beloved, is the truth so raw—
In this life, we face war after war.
But remember, even when the sword swings low,
We rise again, and the victory we'll show.

Is this poetry in motion, or is it poetic justice?

Yours truly,
Lucky Goldie.

Section 3: The Tales of (Chronologically Arranged)

Reflection

Stories that bind us with life's universal lessons- love, growth, loss, and resilience.

Peace, love, and blessings, my beloved family and friends,

A tale of eternal youth, a dance through days gone by,
Where innocence held us close, reaching high to the sky.
In the heart of those youthful years, we dared to believe,
In gifts wrapped in wonder, in dreams we'd retrieve.
We chased every sunrise with laughter and play,
Holding tight to that light, pushing shadows away.

Through the maze of adolescence, in a world painted dark,
We kept our childlike glow, our ember, our spark.
We saw storms on the horizon, clouds heavy with night,
Yet we stood unshaken, embracing pure light.
Even as the years called us forward to grow,
Our spirit stayed gentle, untouched by the flow.
Held tight to that innocence, to the essence of grace,
Our childlike wonder still finds its place.

For what was the test? To keep pure amidst the strife,
In a world that forgets the sweet youth of life.
To hold onto love in a place cold and vast,
Where innocence slips, fades all too fast.
But we made it, beloveds, against all the odds,
Our hearts still young, our souls filled with God's nod.
The gift chose us, and we carry it still,
A blessing wrapped in resilience, strengthened by will.

So here's to us, the ones who passed the test,
No burden, no worry, just feeling blessed.
The moral, my family and friends, is this truth we confess:
We've held onto youth, the world's finest finesse.

Is this poetry in motion, or is it poetic justice?

Yours truly,
Lucky Goldie.

Peace, love, and blessings, my beloved family and friends,

A tale passed down from ancient days,
Of a young lover boy, lost in love's haze.
Fascinated by the essence of desire,
Every glance, every touch, set hearts on fire.
They say his aura was like a magnetic spell,
A gift from the gods, or so the legends tell.

He finessed every moment, every step, every scene,
With words like silk, and eyes that gleamed.
Hundreds of concubines fell at his feet,
For love was his kingdom, and lust his sweet treat.
But what was his sin, why did fate turn cold?
The legend reveals what remains untold.

East and west, from villages far and wide,
Men watched in anger as their wives would slide—
Into his arms, under his gaze,
Blinded by love, lost in his maze.
He bedded the wives of the powerful men,
Not knowing the storm that brewed within.

One fateful night, they came for him fast,
The lover boy's reign had met its last.
Captured by those who couldn't forgive,
For he crossed the line, a dangerous way to live.
They hung him high for the village to see,
His sin? Letting love blind him so recklessly.
Manipulative tactics, seduction's dark art,
No status too high for him to break apart.

And so he swayed, the wind carrying his tale,
Of love gone wrong, of passion turned pale.
His gift, his curse, intertwined as one,
For love gave him power, but left him undone.

The moral, my beloved, in this ancient lore,
Is that love, when twisted, can wound to the core.
Too much finesse, too much desire,
Can lead even the greatest to hang by the fire.

Is this poetry in motion, or is it poetic justice?

Yours truly,

Peace, love, and blessings, my beloved family and friends,

A tale of bravery, from rags to riches,
One man, relentless, pulling himself from the ditches.
Crabs in a barrel, they tried to pull him down,
But with Abba's grace, he turned it all around.
I call it epiphany—she is so sweet to me,
A vision so clear, now it's all up, it's meant to be.

Fear, jealousy, hate—tried to consume,
But like a speed racer, I flew past the gloom.
At the finish line, breaking through the haze,
Out of that pool of misery, I rose in praise.

Into the sea of greatness, I dove deep,
Unshakable, unbreakable, my soul to keep.
I give thanks to Abba, for leading the way,
To my momma and poppa, who molded the clay.

And Brooklyn, NYC—the place that raised me right,
A city of grit, where we learned how to fight.
I stand here now, magnificent and proud,
From the struggle, from the grind, I rose from the crowd.

No longer bound by the crabs in the trap,
I found my path, never looking back.
This mentality, I shattered with might,
The barrel couldn't hold me; I took flight.

By Abbas grace, I see it now clear,
The journey was hard, but there's nothing to fear.
Gratitude fills me for all I possess,
For the struggles, the wins, and the countless tests.

From rags to riches, from broke to elite,
I stand on this mountain with fire in my feet.
The moral is simple, the message is bold—
We rise above it all, with stories untold.

Is this poetry in motion? Or is it poetic justice?
To see where I've been, from struggle to trust—
I give thanks to my city, my family, my faith,
For all that I am, I stand in this grace.

Bless up to my beloved family and friends,
From the start of the story to where it all ends.
Yours truly,
Lucky Goldie.

Peace, love, and blessings, my beloved family and friends,

A tale of a free man, where the story begins.
Fought tooth and nail, bones and soul,
For the sake of our ancestors, enslaved and controlled.

But this here freeman, courageous and strong,
A brave heart who knew right from wrong.
Gave the people hope, faith anew,
Ambitious by nature, to his purpose he flew.

Through faith alone, he led them to the land,
Promised with dew and honey, under God's hand.
Now free from fear, pain, and slavery's chain,
The people rejoiced, no longer in vain.

They sought to worship him, to give him praise,
But he stopped them short, in a powerful blaze.
"My people," he shouted, with voice so clear,
"All glory to ABBA, to Him we revere."

He pointed to the heavens, where the light shines bright,
The people understood, in that sacred sight.
This freeman liberated not by his own hand,
But by ABBA's design, a miracle grand.

Present day speaking, the moral's still true,
He never gave up hope, love, or faith too.
No matter what the father of lies would throw,
This freeman's courage continued to grow.

A stalwart not for one age, but for all,
Standing tall, answering the call.
To be continued, as the story unfolds,
Bless up, family and friends, in the warmth of the soul.

Is this life's rhythm in motion, or divine justice at play?
In the dance of faith and courage, we find our way.

Yours truly,
Lucky Goldie

Peace, love, and blessings, my beloved family and friends,

A tale unfolds in a desert land, where the journey begins.
A man from a village, burdened by strife,
Set off on a mission, to seek a new life.

Twelve miles in, under the scorching sun,
Fatigue set in, his strength undone.
A mirage appeared, or so he thought,
But a genie emerged, with gifts he brought.

"Three wishes I grant, to save your soul,"
The man's heart raced, as he pondered his goal.
"Riches," he wished, "and a long life too,"
But his final request was one few dare to pursue.

He paused, then asked, "Grant me the power,
To understand women, in every hour."
The genie laughed, a chuckle so deep,
"Even I lack that power, not mine to keep."

In shock and disbelief, the man fainted away,
But when he awoke, to his wife he did lay.
Riches and long life, his wishes fulfilled,
Yet understanding women, remained unskilled.

The moral, dear family, is gentle and wise,
Women are delicate, under our skies.
Prone to emotion, sensitive and deep,
As men, we must strive, their hearts to keep.

No genie required, no wish in hand,
Just love and patience, as we take our stand.
For Godspeed guides us, in this life's dance,
Understanding unfolds, if we give it a chance.

Is this poetry in motion, or poetic justice divine?
The journey's the answer, where hearts intertwine.

Yours truly,
Lucky Goldie

Peace, love, and
blessings, my beloved
family and friends,

A tale as old as time, yet it never grows stale,
For the writer's block has crumbled, and I prevail.
It took a minute, but now I'm digging this roll,
Over the essence of victory, it's igniting my soul.

The feeling is lit, too bright to ignore,
I had my epiphany, it opened a door.
32 years upon this earth, a moment so rare,
Lasting a lifetime, a breath of fresh air.

15 minutes of fame, stretched indefinitely,
So the people dem can know my name endlessly.
I play games, but this right here? Ain't no game,
The greatness within us, putting haters to shame.

The moral is simple: I remain the same,
And my beloveds, y'allz know, I will never change.
No matter how small or large the shift,
Just ask my name, and they all will say it swift.

For in this life, as the tides may turn,
My essence stays steady, with lessons we learn.
Is this poetry in motion, or is it poetic justice?
A question to ponder, as we navigate the trust.

Yours truly, Lucky Goldie.

Peace, love, and blessings, my beloved family and friends,

And so, a tale unfolds of an iron-clad soldier,
Supremely fearless in the eyes of men,
But deep inside, he was smothered with love and kindness,
A heart tender, though his exterior was iron-tough, again and again.

Yet, the same sword they knighted him with,
They goodnighted him with—how twisted the fate!
The hate was that real for the supreme one,
A king from the ghetto, with fortune too late.

Fortune forsakes him, his gold turned to dull iron,
But when embraced by LUCK, even iron sharpens to GOLD,
He was nearly crucified for his success,
All because this soldier, this king, refused to be sold.

The ghetto-born king, they envied his rise,
But he escaped the madness, with sanity intact,
Now he stands as the Golden Goose,
Blessed for all his days, that's a fact.

The moral is, my beloved family and friends,
No matter the sword or the hate that descends,
This soldier's spirit is golden, unyielding,
He's not just surviving—he's brilliantly wielding.

Is this poetry in motion, or is it poetic justice?
Bless up, my beloveds, the tale is robust.

Yours truly,
Lucky Goldie.

Peace, love, and blessings, my beloved family and friends,

Let me tell you a tale of the Aquarian winds. For this sign is not just any in the sky, But the luckiest charm, a star lifted high.

In China's old tales, they call it divine, The bearer of waters, the keeper of time. In Arabia, they say fortune flows from this hand, An Aquarian soul is blessed to stand. In African lore, under the sun's grace, The Aquarian stands, untouched by disgrace.

It's no accident I was named Lucky Goldie, My life marked by a fate deep and holy. For my essence is rooted in knowing my worth, In every room, since birth, I knew I belonged to earth.

I walk in a frequency that shimmers and glows, A nature so pure, so wild, it knows. The charm that I carry, the charisma I bring, It's not just by chance—it's a destined thing.

Many walk without ever sensing their own, But fortune found me, and my nature shone. The essence of Aquarius, free and untamed, A wave of luck, by fate proclaimed.

For the highest truth in this life's grand scheme, Is knowing one's essence, one's soul, one's dream. The aura that follows, a gift so rare, Lucky by nature, blessed everywhere.

So may you know your nature, in all that you do, May your spirit ring true, may it guide you through. In every step, in every choice you make, Remember the luck you hold for your own sake.

Is this poetry in motion, or is it poetic justice?

Yours truly,
Lucky Goldie

Peace, love, and blessings, my beloved family and friends,

A tale as old as the first heartbeat, yin and yang collide, Twin forces of balance, where dark and light reside. A dance of shadow and sun, chaos and calm, Opposing, yet woven, in life's eternal psalm. For without the depths, the heights cannot soar, Without the quiet peace, chaos roars even more.

Yin whispers soft, a pull into night's embrace, A reminder that in stillness, we find a sacred place. Cool as the moon's face, steady, and deep, Holding all secrets, the places we keep. A mother to mystery, a keeper of dreams, The quiet that guards us, though silent it seems.

Yang bursts like fire, relentless, unbound, The force that builds mountains, shakes the ground. Bright as the sun's heat, fierce, and alive, Driving us forward, a will to survive. He is power and passion, burning with pride, Yet without yin's restraint, he'd run far and wide.

Together they meet, where twilight touches dawn, A balance unbreakable, though seasons move on. One cannot conquer; they yield, side by side, Two souls in harmony, a limitless tide. They are life's pulse, the rhythm, the song, Teaching us balance, where we all belong.

So remember this, my beloved family and friends, In the ebb and the flow, we find how it blends. The moral here is not to resist or suppress, For balance is power, the world's true finesse.

Is this poetry in motion, or is it poetic justice?

Yours truly,
Lucky Goldie.

Section 4: Strength and Resilience

Reflection

These poems celebrate the strength found in perseverance, courage, and the journey to greatness.

**Peace, love, and
blessings, my beloved
family and friends,**

Don't let 'em tell you what you can't achieve,
Their doubts don't define the blessings you'll receive.
That crab in the barrel mentality is so real,
If they can't see their greatness, they don't want you to feel.
But when you know your worth, made in God's own design,
You walk a different path, one that's truly divine.

Folks will tell you, "If I couldn't do it, neither will you,"
But their fears and their failures don't make your dreams untrue.
See, the truth is, when you're destined for greatness,
You'll rise above their hate, untouched by their fakeness.
Self-hate runs deep, it tries to divide,
But when you walk with purpose, God is your guide.

Don't give up, don't ever give in,
You're made in His image, that's where you begin.
Your goals are yours, your vision is clear,
Block out the noise, the doubt, the fear.
For every setback, there's a comeback waiting,
Every moment of patience is a blessing creating.

The problem ain't the goals we dream or the success we chase,
It's the self-hate that's keeping us from our rightful place.
But when you stand tall, and know who you are,
No one can stop you—you're born to go far.
Made in His image, destined to be great,
You'll rise to the top, no matter how late.

The moral is simple: don't let 'em steer you wrong,
Keep chasing your dreams, stay focused, stay strong.
No matter the doubts, the whispers, or the lies,
Your greatness is yours—just open your eyes.

Is this poetry in motion, or is it poetic justice?

Yours truly,
Lucky Goldie.

Peace, love, and blessings, my beloved family and friends,

We stand on business, no matter what they say,
Relentless, persistent, we carve out our own way.
No for an answer? That's a language we don't speak,
We've spent our lives getting it wrong, but now we seek—

To get it right, to feel the victory in our bones,
This frequency we embrace, it's the strength we've grown.
Through trial and error, through struggle and strife,
We've learned that persistence is the key to this life.

The laws of attraction, they bend to our will,
We attract what we manifest, moving steady, still.
According to the stars, I've witnessed it clear,
The energy we give, returns year after year.

We've seen the doubt, we've faced the lies,
But through it all, we've learned to rise.
From getting it wrong, now we see the light,
We come, we see, and we conquer the fight.

It's a victory, not just in wealth or gain,
But in the persistence that runs through our veins.
This essence, this fire, it's more than just pride,
It's the courage to stand firm, to never hide.

To keep pushing, to keep striving, even when it's tough,
Knowing deep down, our grit is enough.
We've faced the storms, we've weathered the pain,
And now, family and friends, we've broken the chains.

Sensational is the word, for the path that we tread,
Standing on business, with every move we've led.
Not just for us, but for the legacy we leave,
For the ones that follow, for the ones who believe.

The moral is simple: we've embraced the fight,
Stood on business, refused to take flight.
And in that resilience, we've found our might,
This is our victory, shining bright.

Is this poetry in motion? Or is it poetic justice?
For every dream we've chased, every push, every trust—
We've stood tall, relentless, in the face of it all,
And now, my beloved family and friends, we shall never fall.

Yours truly,
Lucky Goldie.

Peace, love, and blessings, my beloved family and friends,

Courage is the armor we wear in this war,
The world throws nightmares, but we dream for more.
They want us smothered in doubt and fear,
But we rise like lions, with vision clear.
Manifesting greatness when they say we can't,
Planting seeds of dreams, growing them giant.

See, the world wants you broken, lost in the haze,
But we turn that darkness into brighter days.
The nightmares try to whisper, "You'll never be free,"
But my faith is unshakable—it's the key.
I manifest my future, I create my own lane,
Turned all of my losses into undeniable gain.

For every door they slam, I break through the walls,
I defy gravity every time I fall.
It's courage, my family, that makes us stand tall,
In the face of defeat, we answer the call.
I've seen the storms, but I've danced in the rain,
For every nightmare, I've turned it into a chain—
A chain of victories, linked by perseverance,
Proof that with courage, there's no interference.

The world may throw shadows, try to smother the light,
But our dreams shine brighter, no matter the fight.
We conquer the fear, the doubt, the confusion,
And rise to the top, making our own conclusion.

The moral is simple, my beloved, stand tall,
Manifest your dreams, even when you fall.
Courage is the key, the weapon of the strong,
It's how we transform the pain into a song.

Is this poetry in motion, or is it poetic justice?

Yours truly,
Lucky Goldie.

Peace, love, and blessings, my beloved family and friends,

Every season has a story,
a reason, a rhythm, a layer of glory.
Some bring heat, some bring cold,
but all are part of the **Seasons of Gold**.

Spring taught me to grow without fear,
Summer taught me to shine and appear.
Fall reminded me to release what's dead,
and Winter taught me how to rest my head.

In all of it—there was purpose,
even when it felt surface.
Even when the leaves fell,
and my spirit felt empty like a broken shell.

But gold ain't made in comfort,
it's forged in fire,
and I've walked through every element
and still rose higher.

These seasons? They sacred.
Marked by tears, by triumphs, by prayers I once faded.
But look at me now—crafted and bold,
wearing every scar like jewelry of old.

So as the winds change and stories unfold,
I embrace each one as a **Season of Gold**.

Is this poetry in motion, or is it poetic justice?
I ask because if life moves in seasons,
then every loss had its reasons,
and every turn was divine alignment in disguise.

Yours truly,
Lucky Goldie

Section 5: Love, Honor, and Loyalty

Reflection

An homage to the enduring power of love, loyalty, and honor, especially in relationships.

Peace, love, and blessings, my beloved family and friends,

Let's speak on a love that never bends or ends.
Love is kind, love is patient, it knows no strife,
It keeps no account of wrongs, it breathes life.

It doesn't get puffed up, no pride in its way,
Behaves with decency, night and day.
It believes all things, endures all storms,
This love is unconditional, in all its forms.

It takes strength, a courage profound,
To love like this, where true hearts are found.
Whether in general or with your significant other,
This love is divine, like no other.

The moral is clear, if God says so,
Then we must follow, let this love flow.
Being made in His image, the truth is plain,
Or is it unseen, to the human brain?

Faith in love, it's what we hope for,
But life can harden us, close the door.
Yet let me tell you, what pierces the wall,
True unconditional love, conquers it all.

Godspeed, my family and friends, we must trust,
In love that never fails, in love that's just.

Is this poetry in motion, or poetic justice divine?
In this love, we find our eternal shine.

Yours truly,
Lucky Goldie

Peace, love, and blessings, my beloved family and friends,

Let's talk about peace, the calm that stills the storm,
The steady hand that guides us, keeps our spirits warm.
In a world that moves so fast, we need a gentle pace,
To honor loyalty and respect, to walk with modest grace.

Love, the mighty force, stronger than steel or stone,
It's what connects us deeply, even when we're alone.
It doesn't boast, it doesn't break, it's patient and it's kind,
It's the thread that weaves our hearts, the treasure that we find.

And then there's honor, the code that lights our way,
To keep our word, to stand up tall, come what may.
It's in the way we treat each other, the way we strive and try,
To hold each other up, to never let a spirit die.

Now let's not forget the queens, the amazing women who reign,
God's wonderful complement to man, through joy and through pain.
When we're feeling low, lost in the depths, down in the mire,
They lift us up, ignite our souls, set our spirits on fire.

They are the hands that hold us steady, the voices that soothe our fears,
The strength behind our courage, the ones who catch our tears.
In their presence, we find solace, in their love, we find our peace,
They are the anchors in our storms, the moments of release.

For every king needs his queen, the balance in the dance,
The one who sees the best in him, who gives him another chance.
They're the calm in our chaos, the light when it gets dim,
The ones who remind us gently, that we are built to win.

So let's honor our women, with respect that knows no end,
For they are the ones who heal us, the lovers, the best friend.
They bring us up when we're down, they hold us close and tight,
They are the essence of our peace, our love, our guiding light.

Is this poetry in motion? Or is it poetic justice's call?
A tribute to the women who stand with us through it all.

Yours truly,
Lucky Goldie.

Peace, love, and blessings, my beloved family and friends,

There's an essence to this aura, star-like and grand,
Born beneath a snow-white moon, perfectly planned.
Whether strutting through a big arena, a grand parade,
Or simply walking in your local bodega's shade.

The presence is felt, surreal and profound,
Goosebumps rise as your feet touch the ground.
This here Aquarian, gifted of the gifted, true,
Strove to stay incognito, behind the scenes, it's what he'd do.

Embracing the shadows, the life of low-key,
Yet co-signing others, roaming this earth freely.
With the same charisma, that lights up the room,
The moral is simple, we walk light in bloom.

We tread softly, not to anger the ground,
For not just one day, but for all our days, sound.
Bless up, family and friends, till the very end,
Let our light shine, as we ascend.

Is this poetry in motion, or is it poetic justice?

Yours truly,
Lucky Goldie.

Section 6: Life's Cycles and Seasons

Reflection

Capturing the ebb and flow of life's cycle, embracing change with grace and gratitude.

Peace, love, and blessings, my beloved family and friends,

Dear Summer, dear winter, where the journey begins.
I promised summer good times, good vibes, in the sun,
Chillin' with all my sons, the fun had just begun.

Okay, did that, now little Ms. Winter, you're next,
Promised her warm nights, cold days, no regrets.
Hot chocolate, lit days, excitement in the air,
The essence of seasons, a balance we share.

Hot sun scorching, life in full blaze,
Winter's cold freeze, takes our breath away.
Mix hot and cold, what do we find?
A lukewarm feeling, where heart and mind align.

Together we rise, together we conquer,
In the mix of extremes, our spirits grow stronger.
I'd rather feel lukewarm, balanced and right,
Than swaying in disarray, from day to night.

Humbling to embrace a frequency so warm,
Steady and true, in life's ever-changing form.
Hot and cold, angry and happy, they collide,
But in lukewarm peace, our souls can glide.

Bless up indefinitely, with love so true,
Finding balance, in all that we do.
Is this poetry in motion, or poetic justice in play?
With Godspeed, we find our way.

Yours truly,
Lucky Goldie

Peace, love, and blessings, my beloved family and friends,

Let's dive deep where the truth begins and ends.
Love, honor, respect, loyalty, peace—they reign,
While hate, jealousy, envy, fear—bring only pain.

Love is a force that lifts us high,
Honor keeps us steady, our heads to the sky.
Respect builds bridges, loyalty binds,
Peace calms the storm in our hearts and minds.

On the other side, there's a different game,
Hate festers, jealousy feeds the flame.
Envy corrodes, fear locks the door,
A world where only money and violence score.

But we, the lover boys and gals, we know the way,
Our courage lights the darkest day.
We rise above with hearts of gold,
In a world so cold, our warmth is bold.

The moral is simple, though the world complex,
God did, so we must follow, step by step.
One day at a time, let love lead,
In this journey of life, that's all we need.

Is this poetry in motion, or poetic justice divine?
We choose love every time, in this world of yours and mine.

Yours truly,
Lucky Goldie

Peace, love, and blessings, my beloved family and friends,

We was winning through the winter, braving the cold,
For spring to feel the gleam, the story we told.
Splashed the cash, 'cause it was coming in fast,
For the summer days ahead, living large, having a blast.

Now it's hot and wavy, smothered in gravy, feeling so fly,
Riding this epiphany, like clouds in the sky.
But enough of the Ra Ra, the loudness, the cheer,
Summer's fading out, now autumn's drawing near.

We walking light, every step that we take,
Through every season, for every blessing's sake.
Enjoying the fall, leaves crisp under feet,
But man, I miss summer, that sweltering heat.

Yet here we are, as little Miss Winter creeps in,
The cycle starts anew, the cold breath of wind.
We running again, but this ain't just a race,
We running towards greatness, catching the pace.

Towards excellence, decadence, with every stride,
In the magnificence of Godspeed, we take pride.
We toast to the seasons, the changes they bring,
The highs and the lows, the songs that we sing.

For every moment, every breath, every win,
Is a blessing, my beloveds, from within.
If you read it, you feel it, you know what I mean,
The moral's in the journey, the spaces in between.

From winter's grip to summer's blaze,
We move through life, in these glorious days.
Bless up to the very end, through thick and thin,
For every end is a new beginning, a chance to begin again.

Is this poetry in motion? Or is it poetic justice?
A celebration of life's cycles, illustrious and robust.

Yours truly,
Lucky Goldie.

Section 7: Reflection on Wealth and Purpose

Reflection

On wealth, purpose, and the wisdom in knowing what truly matters beyond material pursuits.

Peace, love, and blessings, my beloved family and friends,

Let's talk about a truth that never bends.
The love of money—what a dangerous game,
It drives some mad, and puts others to shame.

It's mind-boggling, the evidence so clear,
People sell their souls, fueled by fear.
They screw over loved ones, betray their kin,
Chasing paper, they lose within.

The O'Jays sang it, yet the message is missed,
Knuckleheads still caught up in this twisted bliss.
Money is a tool, not a lover to chase,
In my life, it's business, with a modest face.

The vision, the dream, the master plan,
Guided by wisdom, that's how I stand.
I see the bigger picture, the grand design,
Not blinded by greed, but by faith divine.

No wings on my wealth, it won't fly away,
My eyes are fixed on a brighter day.
Trail and error open eyes to see,
The magnificence the All Father laid out for me.

So let's keep our hearts open, and our faith strong,
Unshakable, unbreakable, where we belong.
Ironclad, Super Saiyan, armored and blessed,
This is Godspeed, at its very best.

Bless up, my beloved family and friends,
In faith and love, our journey never ends.

Is this poetry in motion, or poetic justice divine?

Yours truly,
Lucky Goldie

Peace, love, and blessings, my beloved family and friends,

Fatherhood, a title I wear with pride,
365 days, 366 in a leap, no place to hide.
Striving to cease fear, 'cause life ain't fair,
But we here, standing tall, ready to care.

The beauty of watching your little one grow,
From tiny steps to the big world they'll know.
Little gal or little boy, the joy is profound,
In every laugh, every tear, every little sound.

Wouldn't trade my gift for nada, nothing, not a thing,
Grateful for the peace and love they bring.
They mirror our hopes, reflect our dreams,
In their eyes, the world isn't always what it seems.

A sacred bond, a promise we keep,
Through sleepless nights and dreams so deep.
Guiding them gently, teaching them grace,
Always striving, in life's endless race.

For in every moment, from dawn till dusk,
We build their world on a foundation of trust.
Through ups and downs, in joy and in strife,
Fatherhood's the greatest blessing in life.

The moral here, my beloved, is crystal clear,
To cherish each day, each month, each year.
For I am more than a father; I am their shield,
In the battle of life, my love is the field.

Is this poetry in motion? Or is it poetic justice?
A testament to the journey, so priceless and illustrious.
Bless up, beloveds, to the end of all days,
May these words uplift, in all of our ways.

Yours truly,
Lucky Goldie.

Peace, love, and blessings, my beloved family and friends,

Four and a half years back, I took a vow so deep,
To imitate the Son and the All Father, a promise to keep.
In real time, I embraced the path, humbling my stride,
Seeing others as superior, setting my ego aside.

I reached out, heart open, to those worthy of this grace,
Sharing delicate wisdom, that life's not just a race.
Faithfully, I stuck to the script, with humility in hand,
Navigating through the challenges, striving to understand.

It takes resolve to recognize, in each of us resides the light,
Gifted by the All Father, equal hours in our sight.
I've started to see myself as time, in every breath and glance,
In hindsight, we are time—each moment a chance.

For it's on us, my beloveds, what we make of these hours,
To choose greatness, manifesting dreams, conquering with power.
I choose to be elite, not for fame or wealth's lust,
But to honor the gift of time, a legacy to trust.

The moral here, my family, if you read it, you'll know,
What's understood need not be explained, just let it flow.
For we overstand when wisdom's laid bare, in plain sight,
We rise above confusion, finding clarity in the light.

Consider the seconds, the minutes, the hours we spend,
Are they building us up? Or do they just pretend?
Are we lifting others, like the Son would have done?
Or are we chasing shadows, forgetting the sun?

This journey's about patience, it's about faith and resolve,
To look within, find the truth, and let your soul evolve.
So let's choose to be great, in every breath, every line,
For we are the masters of our own divine time.

Is this poetry in motion? Or is it poetic justice's call?
A reminder that within us lies the potential of it all.

Yours truly,
Lucky Goldie.

Peace, love, and blessings, my beloved family and friends,

Greatness don't always shout—it whispers.
It moves in silence, through cracks in the system.
No fireworks, no grand display,
just purpose unfolding in a humble way.

In the quiet of greatness, I sharpen my soul,
walking light so I don't piss the ground off below.
No need for noise, no hunger for fame,
because the real ones know—it's not just a name.

It's how you show up when nobody sees,
how you stay grounded while chasing dreams.
The still moments, where ego dies,
and only the spirit testifies.

I've seen loud men fall with shaky hands,
while quiet ones rose with God's own plans.
I've prayed in silence, cried without sound,
yet every tear watered this sacred ground.

My story ain't written in bright neon light,
it's carved in stone under starless night.
So if you ask how I became who I became—
just know it was born in the stillness of flame.

Is this poetry in motion, or is it poetic justice?
I ask because the loudest triumphs echo not in noise,
but in the quiet conviction of chosen boys.

Yours truly,
Lucky Goldie

Peace, love, and blessings, my beloved family and friends,

I said it before, I've been here before, where the journey transcends.
The cadence of eliminating distractions, locking self within,
Channeling God's gift, that's where we begin.

Beating the odds, 2 in 92 million, standing tall,
Crab in the barrel mentality, I won't let us fall.
Oh, if I can't do it, you can't either? No bueno!
The art of giving goes beyond, you know.

Not just physically, but in spirit and mind,
Emotionally, we lift each other, truly kind.
Ironclad armor, blessed by the All-Father's hand,
Immune to the pinches of hate, envy, that stand.

No competition, as a son of God,
All deeds righteous, no facade.
The moral here, support and motivate,
Inspire our brothers and sisters, that's our fate.

In a world consumed by so much hate,
We stay unorthodox, setting our own pace.
Don't follow the flow, be the flow,
If they ain't rolling with us, they'll watch us grow.

Step by step, block by block,
We rise together, solid as a rock.
Bless up, family and friends, hold tight,
With Godspeed, we shine our light.

Yours truly,
Lucky Goldie

Section 8: Faith, Legacy, and Guidance

REFLECTION

Anchoring life's journey in faith, leaving a legacy, and staying true to one's purpose.

**Peace, love, and
blessings, my beloved
family and friends,**

The vision is alive, where my journey ascends.
To envision, to see with eyes wide open,
My synergy relentless, through storms unbroken.

Five months left in 2024's stride,
The force from December 31st, still burning inside.
Ambition, my constant, never leaves my side,
Weathering all storms, with God as my guide.

Grateful to possess this divine blessing,
Energy rising, super saiyan progressing.
Held back my words, let the Creator's truth in,
Eye for an eye, skin for skin.

Tooth for tooth, life's stakes are high,
A man will give all, to survive and fly.
The gift from above, keeps giving anew,
I'll share these blessings, with my crew.

Beloved family and friends, grateful I stand,
A steward for God, with love I expand.
The vision's crystal clear, for all my years,
Guided by faith, I conquer my fears.

Is this poetry in motion, or poetic justice at play?
With Godspeed, we find our way.

Yours truly,
Lucky Goldie

Peace, love, and blessings, my beloved family and friends,

This story echoes truths where our history bends. Made in America, woven deep in its land, Four hundred years of chains, forged by hand.

Nearly two centuries have slipped through the years, But look around close, the struggle still steers. Major strides have been made, and our voices now heard, Yet America's past lingers— unspoken, unblurred.

 No formal apology, no mending, no grace, The wounds fester deep with no closure in place. And in that silence, lies feed on our pain, The father of deception thrives in our chains.

This is why legacy matters, why truth must prevail, To carve out a future where our children won't fail. Seeing the bigger picture demands a grand mind, An extraordinary thinker, unafraid of the climb.

For those willing to rise, let's make history real, To heal from within, to teach, to reveal. Written in the stars, our story shines bright— And the Author above turns darkness to light.

Is this poetry in motion, or is it poetic justice?

Yours truly,
 Lucky Goldie

Peace, love, and blessings, my beloved family and friends,

Today, let us talk of faith that never bends. Not in the hands of men who promise and fall, But in the One who sees beyond it all.

From ancient days, tales of faith arose, Passed down through paths that only Abba knows. Men learned to soar, to reach new heights, But still can't conquer their longest night.

It took a century to lift to the sky, Yet death stands firm, no matter how we try. Machines fly, ships roam the sea, But against that fate, there's no victory.

Our fellow man, just flesh and bone, Will look us in our eyes and deceive, unknown. They promise change, they swear they're true, Yet hide intentions, veiled from view.

So why place trust where lies reside? When truth's found in the One who won't hide. Seek truth over schemes that cloud our sight, Seek justice over greed cloaked in night.

Prophecy speaks, steady and clear, That the world's in chaos, but Abba draws near. So let faith root deep, beyond this scene, For in God alone, our spirits lean.

No mortal hand can still that final breath, Only Abba holds the key over death. Seek clarity where the fog is thick, For God's truth shines while men's words trick.

Love over hate, justice over lies, In a world darkened, let faith arise. Today's madness will pass like the rest, But in faith eternal, we find our best.

Is this poetry in motion, or is it poetic justice?

Yours truly,
Lucky Goldie

Peace, love, and blessings, my beloved family and friends,

Here we are, where the tale begins, A war as old as the stars we gaze, Love versus fear, in life's endless maze.

See, I'd rather be loved than feared any day, For love lights a path in the murkiest gray. Love, it's boundless, it heals, it forgives, While fear keeps one caged, afraid just to live.

There's love of a friend, loyal and true, Love of a family that's seen us through. Love of a spouse, tender and near, And love for humanity, fierce and sincere.

Love beats in my heart to the tune of my art, Each line I write, each beat that I start. I express, I release, all that's within, Setting myself free from the lie, from the sin.

For the world loves a lie and loves to deceive, But love is the truth I choose to believe. When hate steps forth, all sharp and loud, Even hate trembles when true love comes around.

So why give into anger, envy, or spite? When love is before us, clear and bright. Love is eternal, ordained by the All-Father's hand, A shelter, a home, a warm piece of land.

Fear keeps us shackled, hidden and low, But love lets us rise, lets our true selves show. And in this battle, love always reign, For love covers all, even the deepest pain.

Is this poetry in motion, or is it poetic justice?

Yours truly,
Lucky Goldie

Acknowledgments

Creating Life is Just a Dream has been a journey of resilience, growth, and love, and I couldn't have done it alone.
To my family, thank you for the endless love and strength you've given me. To my beloved brother, Sheron Michael Linton (MOE), whose spirit and memory inspire every word on these pages you remind me every day of the power of light and legacy. To my parents and loved ones, thank you for nurturing my dreams and being my foundation.
To my friends and mentors, who encouraged me to express and share my words, I'm grateful for your wisdom and insight. You've been the guiding voices that helped shape this collection.
To the readers, thank you for taking the time to step into these pages. May you find something within these poems that speaks to your soul and reminds you of the beauty in every journey.
Bless up,
Lucky Goldie

About The Author

Lucky Goldie, the middle child of nine siblings, was born and raised in the vibrant heart of Brooklyn, New York. Growing up in a bustling family, Lucky always found solace in books, winning school spelling bees and writing contests with a natural gift for words. During the pandemic, his Aquarian nature known for its creativity and deep sense of connection inspired him to pick up a pen and pad and turn to poetry as a way to bring his family closer together. Writing became a way to unite loved ones, ensuring no one felt alone during life's challenging moments. Brooklyn's ever-present energy and diversity have been a constant force of inspiration for Lucky. Coupled with his determined, winning mentality, these experiences shaped his mission to share wisdom, love, and resilience through poetry. Through his words, Lucky Goldie hopes to spread light and love to all of humanity, reminding us that connection and understanding are at the heart of the human experience.
Bless up.

www.ingramcontent.com/pod-product-compliance
Lightning Source LLC
Chambersburg PA
CBHW050521100526
44581CB00002B/64